PRESENTED TO

_____

WITH LOVE FROM

_____

ON

_____

ZONDERKIDZ

Tiny Truths: Wonder & Wisdom
Copyright © 2020 by Tiny Truths, Inc.
Illustrations © 2020 by Tiny Truths, Inc.

Requests for information should be addressed to:
Zonderkidz, 3900 Sparks Drive SE, Grand Rapids, Michigan 49546

ISBN 978-0-310-76954-5 (hardcover)

Art direction: Ron Huizinga
Illustrations: Tim Penner

Printed in Slovenia

FOR

OUR WONDERFUL PARENTS

who taught us these truths
right from the beginning

tiny ♕ truths

WONDER & WISDOM

CREATED BY
❧ JOANNA RIVARD & TIM PENNER ❧

ZONDERkidz

TABLE OF CONTENTS

INTRODUCING
PSALMS

God loves it when we talk with him, and he promises to listen. We can talk to him anywhere and tell him anything. We can tell him about our joy, share our happiness, our sadness, our fears, and our hopes.

The Psalms show us how to express ourselves to God. They are songs, prayers, and poems written by kings, leaders, and musicians (King David is the most famous Psalm writer). Jesus read the Psalms and quoted them often.

The Psalms are full of feelings, honest questions, praise, and wonder—the feeling you have when you find something amazing or when you are curious about how or why things are the way they are.

The more we tell God what is in our hearts, ask him questions, and thank him for all he has given us, the more we find that sense of wonder as we grow to understand who he is and how much he loves us.

SHOUT FOR JOY TO THE LORD, EVERYONE ON EARTH.
WORSHIP THE LORD WITH GLADNESS.
COME TO HIM WITH SONGS OF JOY.
KNOW THAT THE LORD IS GOD.
HE MADE US, AND WE BELONG TO HIM.
WE ARE HIS PEOPLE.
WE ARE THE SHEEP BELONGING TO HIS FLOCK.
GIVE THANKS AS YOU ENTER THE GATES OF HIS TEMPLE.
GIVE PRAISE AS YOU ENTER ITS COURTYARDS.
GIVE THANKS TO HIM AND PRAISE HIS NAME.
THE LORD IS GOOD. HIS FAITHFUL LOVE CONTINUES FOREVER.
IT WILL LAST FOR ALL TIME TO COME.

PSALM 100:1-5

INTRODUCING PROVERBS

When God told King Solomon that he would give him ANYTHING in the world he wanted, Solomon asked for one thing . . . wisdom.

Solomon wrote Proverbs to share the wisdom that God gave him. God's wisdom helps us to live well and love others well. Wisdom is a part of who God is, and it's something he promises to give us if we ask for it and pursue it.

Being wise means knowing what is right and true and living that way. It's important to ask ourselves who we want to become and how we can get there. When we pursue wisdom and love, we are living the way God made us to live and caring about the things God cares about.

If Psalms show us how to live our lives in relationship with God, Proverbs teaches us how God wants us to live—with him, and with those around us. Together, they remind us what it looks like to live the lives we were made for—close to God, loved by him, and loving one another.

LET YOUR EARS LISTEN TO WISDOM.
APPLY YOUR HEART TO UNDERSTANDING.
CALL OUT FOR THE ABILITY TO BE WISE.
CRY OUT FOR UNDERSTANDING.
LOOK FOR IT AS YOU WOULD LOOK FOR SILVER.
SEARCH FOR IT AS YOU WOULD SEARCH FOR HIDDEN TREASURE.
THEN YOU WILL UNDERSTAND HOW TO HAVE RESPECT FOR THE LORD.
YOU WILL FIND OUT HOW TO KNOW GOD.
YOU WILL UNDERSTAND WHAT IS RIGHT AND HONEST AND FAIR.
YOU WILL UNDERSTAND THE RIGHT WAY TO LIVE.
YOUR HEART WILL BECOME WISE.
YOUR MIND WILL DELIGHT IN KNOWLEDGE.

PROVERBS 2:2–5, 9–10

MY SON, DO NOT FORGET MY TEACHING.
KEEP MY COMMANDS IN YOUR HEART.
DON'T LET LOVE AND TRUTH EVER LEAVE YOU.
TIE THEM AROUND YOUR NECK.
WRITE THEM ON THE TABLET OF YOUR HEART.
THEN YOU WILL FIND FAVOR AND A GOOD NAME
IN THE EYES OF GOD AND PEOPLE.

PROVERBS 3:1, 3–4

GOD MADE EVERYTHING

The beginning of a story is a very important place. And OUR story has an amazing beginning.

The Psalms tell us that before anything else existed, God spoke into the darkness. And all of creation answered.

The whole universe started to unfold at the sound of God's voice, like an incredible conversation between the creator and his creation. Immense mountains, crashing oceans, and towering trees appeared. Flowers, fruits, and vegetables in every shape and color began to grow and multiply.

Countless stars stretched across the moonlit sky while the sun gave warmth and light to the day. Millions of weird, beautiful, and amazing creatures were born into the land and sea.

Life poured from God's loving, wild, and wonderful imagination.

So when you see something amazing and it makes you feel excited, remember that creation—in all of its beauty, wildness, and goodness—is one way that we can understand what God is like, because he made it all.

PSALM 33:6

THE HEAVENS WERE MADE WHEN THE Lord COMMANDED IT TO HAPPEN.
ALL THE STARS WERE CREATED BY THE BREATH OF HIS MOUTH.

GOD MADE YOU

God made the WHOLE universe! That means God made you too.

He made you to be his child and to be loved by him forever. Because we are his children, God delights in us and knows everything about us.

He knows what makes you happy and what makes you sad.

He knows what scares you and what excites you.

In fact, he knew everything about you before you were even born. The Psalms say that God planned and put together every little part of you.

This means he knows you better (and loves you more) than anyone else.

There will always be some things about God that are a mystery to us. But because God made you, nothing about you is a mystery to God.

PSALM 139:13–14

YOU CREATED THE DEEPEST PARTS OF MY BEING. YOU PUT ME TOGETHER INSIDE MY MOTHER'S BODY. HOW YOU MADE ME IS AMAZING AND WONDERFUL. I PRAISE YOU FOR THAT. WHAT YOU HAVE DONE IS WONDERFUL. I KNOW THAT VERY WELL.

GOD IS ALWAYS WITH US

There's nothing God has made that he doesn't know, love, or care for.

God is close to his creation, and he is always close to us.

He is with you when you sleep and when you wake up. He is with you wherever you go and whatever you do.

There is nowhere we can go to escape from God and his great love for us— not high in the mountains . . .

. . . far away across the ocean . . .

. . . or in the darkest hiding place.

King David wrote in the Psalms that nothing can take us away from God—not even how we feel. No anger, sadness, fear, or anything else can separate us from his love.

And if God is always with us, then we are never alone.

PSALM 139:7–8, 10

HOW CAN I GET AWAY FROM YOUR SPIRIT? WHERE CAN I GO TO ESCAPE FROM YOU? IF I GO UP TO THE HEAVENS, YOU ARE THERE. IF I LIE DOWN IN THE DEEPEST PARTS OF THE EARTH, YOU ARE ALSO THERE . . . YOUR HAND WOULD ALWAYS BE THERE TO GUIDE ME. YOUR RIGHT HAND WOULD STILL BE HOLDING ME CLOSE.

WHEN LIFE IS DIFFICULT

King David sang to God when he was happy and he also sang when he was sad. He knew that God was close to him when he felt brokenhearted or scared.

It's a brave thing to be honest about our sadness and our fears. It's important because difficult times, like storms, come to all of us.

The world is broken and there are lots of things that need healing. Sometimes that includes us and our lives, or the lives of people we know.

We won't always understand why painful things happen to us or to anyone else. What we do know is that while there may be storms, God is always bigger than those storms.

God promises to be close to anyone whose heart is broken or sad. Although that might not change the difficult things, knowing it helps us get through them.

And we can help each other through difficult times. God has given us his love to share with one another.

Even in the hardest moments, we can remind each other and remember that God is with us. We are not alone, and we are loved.

PSALM 34:18

THE LORD IS CLOSE TO THOSE WHOSE HEARTS HAVE BEEN BROKEN.

GOD IS WORTHY OF PRAISE

God is so vast and wonderful that we can't ever know everything about him. Which means we get to spend our whole lives discovering more about who he is and what he is like!

There are lots of things we DO know about God. We know that he is kind and strong, loving and faithful, tender, forgiving, and full of joy.

We know that he delights in us and that he never changes. We know that he is good and that he is good to us. We know that he made the earth and the skies and everything in between.

The Bible says something wonderful about everything God has made—it says that ALL of creation worships him. Everything he has created praises him, because everything (in its own way) knows that he deserves our praise.

Because we're part of his creation too, and because we are made for him, our hearts are made to worship God—it's a part of who we are.

God is the creator of all things, the maker of heaven and earth, and the one who loves us with a love that never fails.

He is worthy of our praise!

PSALM 145:3

LORD, YOU ARE GREAT. YOU ARE REALLY WORTHY OF PRAISE.
NO ONE CAN COMPLETELY UNDERSTAND HOW GREAT YOU ARE.

GOD HEARS OUR PRAYERS

When we talk to God we remember that he cares for us, that our hearts are made to be connected to him, and that we are not alone.

God knows everything about us, and he already knows what we need. But he loves it when we come to him, and he wants us to share our thoughts with him because that keeps us close to him.

When we pray we can say anything to God. It's a time to be thankful and a time to say sorry for things we have done wrong. It's a time to think of others and to ask for help.

Sometimes when we pray we get an answer we hoped for, and sometimes we don't. Sometimes we have to wait patiently and listen.

Talking with God can change our hearts because when we are close to him, it reminds us of what is important (and what isn't).

We start to love what God loves and long for the things that he longs for—things like justice and peace, compassion and kindness.

The Psalms tell us that God is always ready to listen and that he hears every prayer. All we need to do is come to him.

PSALM 65:2
ALL PEOPLE WILL COME TO YOU, BECAUSE YOU HEAR AND ANSWER PRAYER.

REMEMBER WHAT GOD HAS DONE

There is so much that God has given us. But sometimes we forget the story of what he has done in our lives.

In the Bible, God told his people many times that he loved them and would take care of them. Still, they often forgot his promises and even forgot his love.

But telling stories and singing songs about what God had already done for them helped God's people to remember what he is like—that he is good and loving. Those stories gave his people hope when life was difficult or confusing.

David tells the most famous of these stories in the Psalms, a story of an impossible rescue. God had helped his people to escape from Egypt and brought them to the wonderful new land he had promised them.

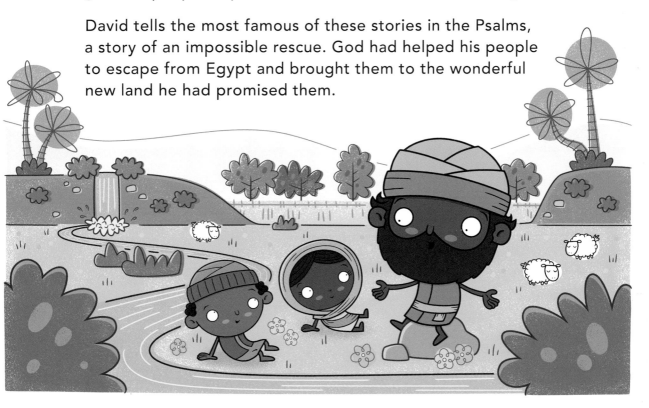

When they told this story to each other, God's people remembered that no matter how they felt, God was faithful (which means he never gives up on us).

We can do the same thing by remembering and sharing what God has done for us and by reading the Bible to remind ourselves that God never changes.

PSALM 103:2

I WILL PRAISE THE LORD. I WON'T FORGET ANYTHING HE DOES FOR ME.

KEEPING GOD IN OUR THOUGHTS

God wants our whole lives to be spent walking with him.

Because God is present in his creation, he is everywhere and always with us. That means that we can talk to him all through the day. In everything we do, God should be in our thoughts.

The things we see around us—in each other and in creation—all show us something of God, because we live in a world that was made by him. So when we walk through our lives with our eyes really open, thinking about how good God is, we will see that there is SO much God wants to show us, SO much he has to teach us, and SO much that he has given us.

King David wrote in the Psalms that he loved to think about God—day and night. He remembered the things that God had done and was grateful for his rules. There is joy in living our lives the way God wants us to.

If we keep God in our thoughts in everything we do, and if we spend time thinking about how God wants us to live, we will find ourselves closer to him. We will have a sense of wonder at everything he has done for us, and we will see more of God in our lives and in the world around us.

PSALM 119:27

HELP ME UNDERSTAND HOW YOUR RULES DIRECT ME TO LIVE. THEN I MAY THINK DEEPLY ABOUT THE WONDERFUL THINGS YOU HAVE DONE.

OUR DAILY BREAD

When Jesus taught us how to pray he told us to ask God for our daily bread. That means asking only for what we need today.

It's normal to wonder about the future, but the Bible says we don't need to worry. In fact, it says that worrying never helps anything!

When we don't worry about tomorrow we are free to enjoy what God has given us today—we can take delight in everything around us! We can be thankful for what we have right now.

Proverbs tells us that all we should ask God for is just what we need each day (which probably isn't much!). If we have too much, we might forget that we need God and his help. We might think we can do everything by ourselves.

If we have too little, we might forget that God has promised to give us what we need and try to solve our problems on our own (in a way that isn't best).

Jesus also knew that when we worry about ourselves (however much or little we have), we can't take care of others. When we worry it's easy to forget that God has promised to look after us AND that he wants us to take care of others too.

Instead of worrying, we can be thankful for whatever we have.

God knows just what we need, and Proverbs reminds us that is all we need to ask for.

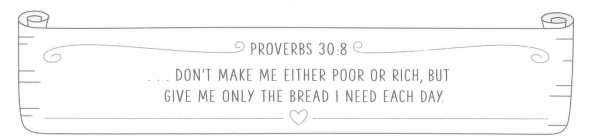

PROVERBS 30:8

. . . DON'T MAKE ME EITHER POOR OR RICH, BUT
GIVE ME ONLY THE BREAD I NEED EACH DAY.

TRUST IN GOD

King David was a good king. He loved God and cared for his people. Being the king of God's people wasn't an easy job. David had lots of questions, lots of difficult times, and lots of enemies. But David trusted God because he knew that God was good.

 And that gave David hope.

In the Psalms, David wrote that because he trusted God, he felt like a strong, healthy olive tree with roots that were holding him up. A healthy tree won't be knocked down by strong winds.

It stays strong and continues to grow.

That's how we can feel too, when we trust God—like a strong, rooted tree, no matter what happens.

Like David, we all have questions about our lives from time to time. When we know that God is for us, and when we obey him, we can trust that the story of our life will grow into something beautiful and strong.

So when you have questions, worries, or fears, remember that God is who he says he is—he is good and faithful, loving, strong, and kind.

He is worthy of our trust.

⟩ PROVERBS 3:5-6 ⟨

TRUST IN THE LORD WITH ALL YOUR HEART. DO NOT DEPEND ON YOUR OWN UNDERSTANDING. IN ALL YOUR WAYS OBEY HIM. THEN HE WILL MAKE YOUR PATHS SMOOTH AND STRAIGHT.

GOD GUIDES OUR PATH

Our lives are like a long, wonderful journey. The best thing about this journey is that we are never alone, because God promises to be our companion and our guide. He walks beside us and helps us choose good paths to be on.

God wants us to think carefully about how we move through our lives, and he promises to help us do that. In Proverbs, he promises to teach us and give us good advice. The Psalms say that when we are close to God he can guide us. We can listen to him and understand how he wants us to live.

The Psalms also say that it's when we are close to God that we find life and joy, even when our path is difficult. So when life brings us decisions to make or choices to consider, we don't need to be anxious. We can trust that God will give us the wisdom we need and that he will help us—because he has said he will.

When we move thoughtfully and wisely through our lives, remembering that we are not alone, we will find joy in the journey and in the everyday.

We were made to walk through life with God at our side, and he promises to be with us as we travel along his paths.

PSALM 32:8

I WILL GUIDE YOU AND TEACH YOU THE WAY YOU SHOULD GO.
I WILL GIVE YOU GOOD ADVICE AND WATCH OVER YOU WITH LOVE.

THE LORD IS MY SHEPHERD

Because God is so vast and wonderful and bigger than anything we can fully imagine, we sometimes use pictures to understand who he is and what he is like. All through the Bible God is described as a good shepherd.

Shepherds needed to be strong protectors, keeping wild animals away from their sheep. They also had to watch over the sheep and guide them, sometimes through dangerous places.

The shepherd stayed with his sheep and they knew his voice. The safest place for the sheep was always close to the shepherd.

David was a powerful king with an army to lead and battles to fight. But when he thought about God, it wasn't just as a strong ruler. His God was also tender and gentle. He was loving. David knew that he was loved and cared for. He knew he was watched over and known.

The same is true for us—God is our shepherd, too, and whatever life looks like, he is always there to watch over us and guide us. He knows exactly what we need and he cares for us. It's important to listen for his voice and stay close to him.

PSALM 23:1–2

THE LORD IS MY SHEPHERD. HE GIVES ME EVERYTHING I NEED.
HE LETS ME LIE DOWN IN FIELDS OF GREEN GRASS.
HE LEADS ME BESIDE QUIET WATERS.

GOD WATCHES OVER US

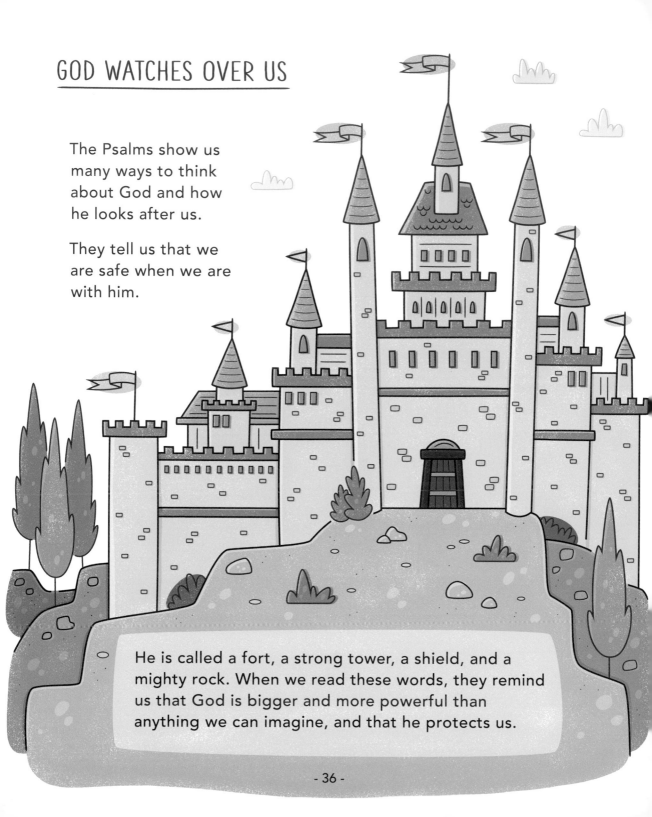

The Psalms show us many ways to think about God and how he looks after us.

They tell us that we are safe when we are with him.

He is called a fort, a strong tower, a shield, and a mighty rock. When we read these words, they remind us that God is bigger and more powerful than anything we can imagine, and that he protects us.

But the Psalms also tell us that God is not just strong and powerful, but tender and caring too. He is a shelter and a refuge; a safe place that we can go to whenever we want. He is like a mother bird who hides and protects her young underneath her wings. He holds us close. That's a wonderful thing to remember when we are feeling anxious or afraid.

The Psalms tell us that God watches over our lives with love. When we take refuge and stay close to him, it's easier for us to keep ourselves from harm and remember how to live wisely.

We all feel scared or anxious at times, but God promises us that whenever we feel lost or afraid he offers us his shelter.

God is our refuge when we need one, and a safe place to be.

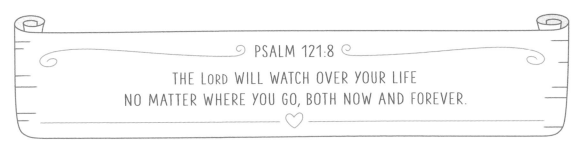

PSALM 121:8
THE LORD WILL WATCH OVER YOUR LIFE
NO MATTER WHERE YOU GO, BOTH NOW AND FOREVER.

ENOUGH FOR EVERYONE

In the Bible, God promised his people that he would always take care of them. He wanted them to be a different kind of tribe from all the others. They would care for everyone as God had cared for them. So he gave them rules to make sure that everyone had enough.

God told his people to leave the edges of their fields unharvested so that anyone from anywhere who was hungry would always be able to find food. Taking care of others was a way of sharing God's love with them, whichever tribe they belonged to.

The Psalms remind us that God is always on the side of the weak and suffering. He cares for the poor and needy. They are precious to him. God wants us to live the same way today—to share whatever we have and make sure that everyone has enough.

God has a heart for those in need. When we care for each other, we honor God and find joy.

PROVERBS 14:31

. . . ANYONE WHO IS KIND TO THOSE IN NEED HONORS GOD.

BE GENEROUS

Generosity is at the heart of who God is—everything we have is a gift from him. The Bible tells us that God's gifts are so amazing we can't even imagine how wonderful they really are.

Because God made us, his generosity is a part of us too.

When we live generously, we remind ourselves that EVERYTHING we have comes from God. That brings us joy and reminds us to be grateful for what we have.

Being generous can change people around us as well.

When we live generous lives, there are always good surprises. Maybe we bring a little more joy into the world today. Maybe we find we can live with less than we thought. Maybe we show someone that they are important. Maybe we cheer someone up. Maybe we remind someone they are not alone.

When we take what God has given us (whatever that might be) and share it generously and joyfully, we're putting more of God's love into the world.

PROVERBS 21:26

. . . GODLY PEOPLE GIVE WITHOUT HOLDING BACK.

LOVE YOUR ENEMIES

There are lots of things in the Bible that sound surprising to us. That's because God wants our story to be a very different one. He shows us a completely new, different way to live.

The Bible tells us many times that we should love our neighbors. It also tells us that we should love our enemies. But even that's not enough for God! Proverbs says that if someone who is our enemy needs help, we should help them. That's not the way many people choose to live, but it IS God's way.

Do you remember the Good Samaritan? Jesus told a story about a man who desperately needed help one day.

The people who should have helped him walked straight past and ignored him.

The one who stopped (the ONLY one who didn't walk past) was someone his tribe hated—a Samaritan. He was the unexpected hero who saw his enemy in need and stopped to help him.

God wants us to be like the Samaritan in Jesus' story—to help even the people who are unkind to us, treat us badly, or just seem hard to love.

He wants us to live lives so full of his extravagant, surprising loving kindness that we love everyone, whoever they are.

PROVERBS 25:21

IF YOUR ENEMY IS HUNGRY, GIVE HIM FOOD TO EAT.
IF HE IS THIRSTY, GIVE HIM WATER TO DRINK.

DON'T BE QUICK TO ANGER

God isn't surprised by our feelings, however strong they are. He made us! He knows exactly what we are feeling, whether we're upset, joyful, anxious, or excited.

So God understands when we feel angry. It's normal to get upset, and even King David wrote lots of Psalms full of angry feelings toward his enemies.

But although God wants us to express anything and everything to him, he also gives us the ability to choose how we respond to our feelings. We need to think about how we act, because our actions can affect so many things around us.

Our small acts of love can repair the world around us, but our anger can break things—it can hurt other people and it can also hurt us. When we hold on to our anger, it becomes a part of us.

But when we choose to respond to anger with grace, peace, and kindness, we bring healing instead of hurt.

Because we are made in God's image, we are made to love. Proverbs tells us that when we forgive and control our anger, we will find peace for ourselves and for others.

PROVERBS 14:30

A PEACEFUL HEART GIVES LIFE TO THE BODY.

WATCH YOUR WORDS

Proverbs tells us that our words have incredible power.

Our words, spoken in love, have the power to encourage others, to cheer people up, to make someone laugh, to remind another of who they are—that they are loved. Our words can heal and mend all kinds of brokenness and sadness.

But the Bible warns us that our words also have the power to hurt others. In fact, Proverbs says that words spoken carelessly can cut like a sword—which means we need to take our words very seriously and choose them wisely.

So be thoughtful when you choose your words, and remember they have great power—to hurt or to heal.

Proverbs says that kind words are like honey—they are sweet and bring healing to the body. The next time you see someone who is sad or upset, remember that your words can make a great difference to them.

PROVERBS 12:18
THE WORDS OF THOUGHTLESS PEOPLE CUT LIKE SWORDS.
BUT THE TONGUE OF WISE PEOPLE BRINGS HEALING.

BE A PEACEMAKER

Everything God does comes from love. And we are made to live in exactly the same way, no matter what situation we find ourselves in.

One way we can do that is by being a peacemaker.

There are lots of ways to be a peacemaker in the world. Some are big, and some are small and quiet. They are all important.

Proverbs tells us that it's foolish to be quick to argue. We should never start fights. We should always try our very best to live at peace with EVERYONE.

When we see people who are upset with each other, sometimes we can help find a solution. God has given you a mind that is full of creative ideas and ways to do things differently.

Sometimes people will be unkind or hurtful to us, or will act without patience. When that happens, we can respond in love instead of anger.

Even helping someone who is lonely, scared, worried, or sad is being a peacemaker. By encouraging them or offering them help, we can bring them peace.

God's peace brings us closer to each other and reminds us what we are made for—a life of togetherness and harmony where we love and are loved.

Imagine what our world would look like if EVERYONE tried their best to respond to one another in peace and love, no matter what.

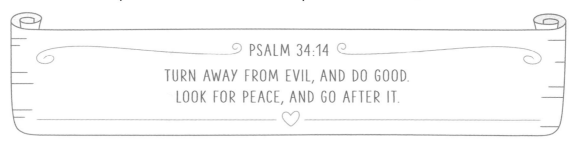

PSALM 34:14

TURN AWAY FROM EVIL, AND DO GOOD.
LOOK FOR PEACE, AND GO AFTER IT.

REFLECTING GOD'S LOVE

In the Bible, God often uses one person to bless another, or one tribe to bless another tribe. He uses us to share his love with others.

That's why he set his people apart to be different from all the other tribes and to live in a different way. God gave Moses rules for a new way of living and told him that if his people kept the rules, he would bless them and others would see and understand who he was.

God was using their lives to tell a different story—to tell the tribes around them about a God who was loving and caring, who knew the needs of his people, who was safe and offered them refuge in difficult times. He was a strong, rescuing God.

People learned these things through watching the lives of God's people, and seeing how he cared for them. They heard stories about this strong God who loved his people.

Today, when we share what we have been given (whether it's what we have or who we are), we are living in the same way. That's how God tells his story through our lives. When we live well and love others well, people will see and understand who God is. He is love!

When we bless those around us, they too can see that God is good.

⌐ PSALM 67:1-2 ⌐

GOD, HAVE MERCY ON US AND BLESS US. MAY YOU BE PLEASED WITH US. THEN YOUR WAYS WILL BE KNOWN ON EARTH. ALL NATIONS WILL SEE THAT YOU HAVE THE POWER TO SAVE.

♡

FRIENDSHIP

Friends are one of the best gifts God gives us.

When life is good, friends celebrate with us and share in our joy. When life is difficult and trouble comes, we need good friends alongside us to help us keep going.

Proverbs tells us something amazing about friendship—it says we become like the people we choose to spend our time with. Which means that we can choose who we are becoming!

If we look around us and find friends who are loving and curious, kind, generous, peaceful, joyful and encouraging, compassionate and wise, we will start to become those things too!

It also means that if we don't like the path we are on, we might need to find different friends. Proverbs says that if we choose friends who are angry, unkind, or selfish, we may start to become like them. So we need to choose our friends well and make sure that we are helping each other in the right direction.

As we journey together through life, good friends keep us company, encourage us, and remind us of who we are and what we are made for. So pick good friends and be a good friend.

⟳ PROVERBS 13:20 ⟲

WALK WITH WISE PEOPLE AND BECOME WISE.

♡

BE HUMBLE

Every single person in our world is valuable, precious, and made in God's image. Sometimes we forget that and think that we're more important than others.

And sometimes we believe certain people are more valuable than others.

But God wants us to see things differently.

Jesus spent a lot of time with people whom others disliked or thought were unimportant.

He saw people for exactly who they were. Each one of them was precious to him and he loved them all equally because we are all God's children. We should live that way too!

In fact, Jesus says we should always put others first—that's what it means to be humble (and it's one big way we share God's love).

When we treat others as valuable (and don't see ourselves as more important than anyone else), we are loving the way God wants us to.

PROVERBS 11:2

. . . WISDOM COMES TO THOSE WHO ARE NOT PROUD.

OTHERS HELP US GROW

When we live our lives with God, we will find that we are always changing, always growing, always learning, and always becoming something new.

In fact, if we look around us at all of creation, we will see that God loves change, growth, new life, and new beginnings. Small things become giant things. Tiny seeds grow into enormous trees.

And he has made us so that we can always learn, change, and grow. But to grow into the people we want to be, we will often need advice and correction from those who love us.

In fact, Proverbs tells us that we can only grow in wisdom and love by looking for that guidance and discipline.

One of the gifts God gives us is people around us who can correct us and guide us along the way. They may be parents or grandparents, aunts and uncles, teachers or neighbors. Throughout your life you will meet different people who have wisdom that will help you stay on a good path.

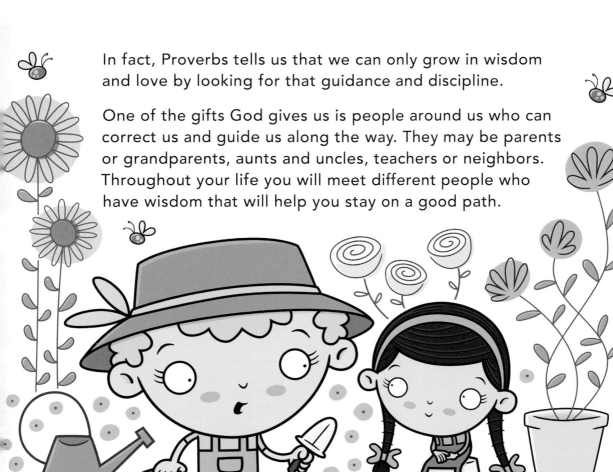

So when people who love you offer you wise words and advice, pay attention! Proverbs says you should get all the advice and instruction you can. That's how you grow in wisdom and love.

PROVERBS 19:20

LISTEN TO ADVICE AND ACCEPT CORRECTION. IN THE END YOU WILL BE COUNTED AMONG THOSE WHO ARE WISE.

FORGIVENESS

In the big story of the Bible, God shows us what it looks like to love unconditionally (which means nothing we do will ever change his love for us).

He also shows us what forgiveness looks like. The Bible promises that no matter what we do, God is always ready to forgive us when we ask him to.

Because we are made in God's image, we are made to love the way God loves. That means we need to forgive the way he forgives. Which isn't always easy, but Jesus says we must learn to do it over and over again.

Although forgiving is something we do, it's actually a gift we give. Proverbs tells us that when we forgive others, it brings freedom and peace to the person we forgive—AND to us! It brings the possibility of a new beginning.

So always forgive and always ask for forgiveness. We love because we are loved. And we forgive because we are forgiven.

PROVERBS 10:12

HATE STIRS UP FIGHTS.
BUT LOVE ERASES ALL SINS BY FORGIVING THEM.

GOD SEES OUR HEARTS

God made us and knows EVERYTHING about us. He sees our hearts and our minds and knows what is happening inside us. He sees when we are full of love, and he knows when we are full of anger. He knows when we are full of a mixture of feelings all scrambled up together.

Proverbs tells us that our actions come from whatever is inside us. What we have in our hearts matters. Like a stream that flows from a bubbling spring, our whole lives (our thoughts, actions, and words) flow from our hearts.

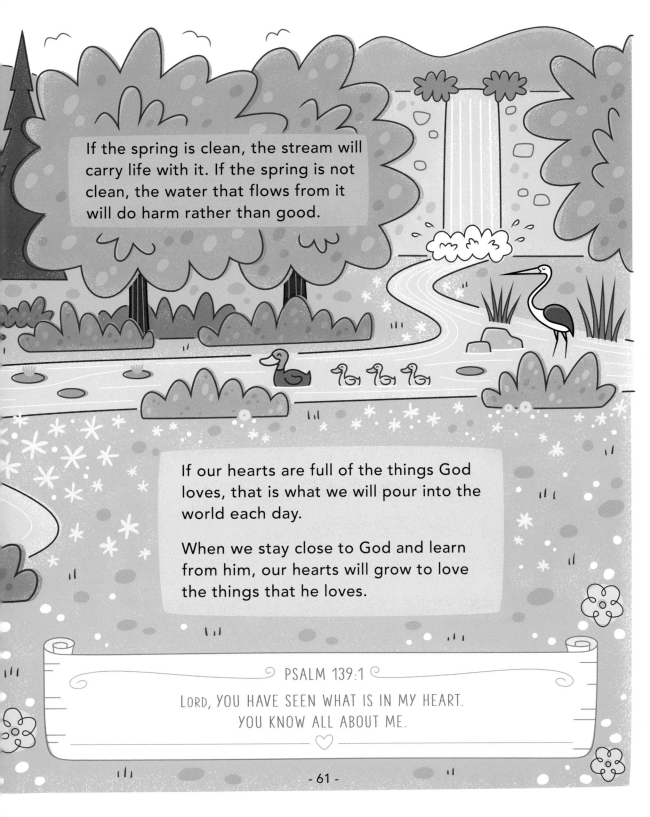

If the spring is clean, the stream will carry life with it. If the spring is not clean, the water that flows from it will do harm rather than good.

If our hearts are full of the things God loves, that is what we will pour into the world each day.

When we stay close to God and learn from him, our hearts will grow to love the things that he loves.

PSALM 139:1

LORD, YOU HAVE SEEN WHAT IS IN MY HEART. YOU KNOW ALL ABOUT ME.

BE STILL AND KNOW

We live in a world that is full of activity, bustle, noise, and movement—a world that doesn't often slow down or quiet down.

But sometimes it's important to stop, slow down, be still and quiet. It's in the stillness that we can hear what God has to say to us. In the quiet we can remember who he is.

Even Jesus knew that he needed to spend time in the quiet places, to be close to God and to pray.

Sometimes when we feel anxious, too busy, or overwhelmed, it's because we haven't taken the time to slow down, find some quiet, and remember what matters (and what doesn't).

When we are calm, we can remember what is true. When we are quiet, we can listen for God's voice and hear what he has to say.

God offers us peace and quiet rest when we come to him.

PSALM 46:10

. . . "BE STILL, AND KNOW THAT I AM GOD."

CARING FOR CREATION

The Bible tells a story of God as a creator who loves what he has made. In the very first story of the Bible, in the book of Genesis, God declares out loud that his creation—all of it—is very good!

So our story begins with a world in which everything has its place, and every created thing has what it needs to flourish and grow.

God cares for his creation.

The Psalms say that God gives water to wild animals and to the birds that sing in the trees. He waters the mountains with rain, making grass grow for the animals to eat, and plants for people to take care of and eat. This is how God takes delight in his creation and provides everything it needs.

The story of the Bible shows us that God's heart is for a world in which everything can grow and flourish as it was made to do. We now live in a world in which not everything or everyone flourishes. We need to care for the things that God cares for. That means taking care of one another and taking care of the world around us.

There are so many ways that we can help to repair and protect the gift of God's creation. It all belongs to him, and we get to help him take care of it.

⟲ PSALM 47:7 ⟳

GOD IS THE KING OF THE WHOLE EARTH.
SING A PSALM OF PRAISE TO HIM.

GOD LOVES WHAT IS RIGHT AND FAIR

The Bible tells us that God hears the cries of those who need help. His heart is always for what is right and fair for everyone.

He heard the cries of his people when they were slaves in Egypt and brought them into freedom. They knew that he was a rescuing God. And he is the same today—a God who hears the cries of those who feel weak or powerless or who have no one to help them.

If we feel there is no hope in our lives, or if we feel powerless or ignored, the Bible reminds us that God is the one who will bring us out of our hopelessness, just as he brought his people out of slavery in Egypt and into freedom.

If we see others who live without hope, or who suffer because they are helpless or powerless or poor, then God wants us to stand up for what is right and fair for EVERYONE. This is how we can bring more of God's love into the world.

God loves what is right and fair. He is a God who rescues those who need him so they can rescue others.

PSALM 33:5

THE LORD LOVES WHAT IS RIGHT AND FAIR.
THE EARTH IS FULL OF HIS FAITHFUL LOVE.

GOD IS FAITHFUL

The Bible is the story of God's faithfulness to us.

Being faithful means never giving up. God's faithfulness means that his love for us will never fail. It means we can ALWAYS trust him. He never changes and he keeps his promises.

Do you remember God's amazing promise to Abraham? God promised Abraham that he and Sarah would have a baby, even though they were both incredibly old. And through Abraham's family God would bless all the nations of the world.

It was an enormous and hard-to-believe promise. But Abraham trusted God because he knew that God is faithful and good, and always does what he says he will.

Over and over again, God keeps the promises he makes to his people. He never gives up on them, even when they don't trust him. Even when they walk away from him.

Because we know that God doesn't change, we know that he is just as faithful to us today as he was to Abraham, Moses, David, and all the people who came after them. The God of Abraham is our God too.

That means we can be confident that God's promises are true and his faithfulness is never-ending.

PSALM 33:4

WHAT THE LORD SAYS IS RIGHT AND TRUE.
HE IS FAITHFUL IN EVERYTHING HE DOES.

JOY

Joy is our natural reaction to understanding who God is and how much he has done for us. Joy is deeper than happiness and stronger than excitement. There might still be sadness, but even out of that sadness can come joy when we go through it together.

It is understanding the truth of who we are: we belong to the God who made all of creation. We are known and loved by him. There is joy when we are close to God.

Psalms and Proverbs show us that when we live the life we are made to live—a life of relationship, compassion, and forgiveness—we will find joy.

Remembering and celebrating all that God had done for them made the Psalm writers sing for joy and write songs full of grateful praise. Our lives should be full of that praise too!

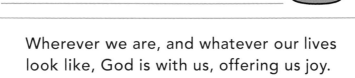

Wherever we are, and whatever our lives look like, God is with us, offering us joy.

○ PSALM 65:8 ○

EVERYONE ON EARTH IS AMAZED AT THE WONDERFUL THINGS YOU HAVE DONE. WHAT YOU DO MAKES PEOPLE FROM ONE END OF THE EARTH TO THE OTHER SING FOR JOY.

♡

GOD IS LOVE

The Psalms tell us that God's love is higher than the heavens. His holiness is as great as the height of the highest mountains. He is as honest as the oceans are deep. He cares for people and animals. God's faithful love is priceless, and it will never fail or change. There is nothing in all of creation that is more valuable or precious than God's love for us. Love is who God is. It's not just at the heart of who he is, it IS who he is!

Through all the stories of the Bible and in our own lives, we see God's faithful and forgiving love. And from that love flows all new life and new creation—second chances and new beginnings.

The great story of the Bible tells us who God is, and it also tells us who we are. God made us to be close to him—to love and be loved. That's what we are made for!

Always remember who you are
and who God truly is.

God is love!

GIVE THANKS

God's gift to us is everything. It's a gift so extravagant that it's impossible to describe it all.

It's life itself. It's God's loving kindness toward us. It's his wisdom and a new way to live. It's forgiveness and the promise of peace and joy. It's a role in the healing of the world. It's a sense of wonder when we look at creation around us.

It's understanding that we are loved, understood, and known. It's knowing that we belong—that we are connected to each other and to God. It's understanding that we are never alone.

ALL of this—all of everything that we have—is a gift. And we know that God delights in giving it to us.

There are two good responses to a gift. One is to enjoy what we are given—to appreciate it and not waste a single drop of it. Living that way brings joy to the gift giver. The other response is simply to give thanks. To say thank you. Again and again.

I WILL SPEND TIME THINKING ABOUT YOUR WONDERFUL DEEDS.
THEY SPEAK ABOUT THE POWERFUL AND WONDERFUL THINGS YOU DO.
I WILL TALK ABOUT THE GREAT THINGS YOU HAVE DONE.
THEY CELEBRATE YOUR GREAT GOODNESS.
THEY SING FOR JOY ABOUT YOUR HOLY ACTS.

THE LORD IS GRACIOUS, KIND AND TENDER.
HE IS SLOW TO GET ANGRY AND FULL OF LOVE.
THE LORD IS GOOD TO ALL.
HE SHOWS DEEP CONCERN FOR EVERYTHING HE HAS MADE.
LORD, ALL YOUR WORKS PRAISE YOU.
YOUR FAITHFUL PEOPLE PRAISE YOU.
THEY TELL ABOUT YOUR GLORIOUS KINGDOM.
THEY SPEAK ABOUT YOUR POWER.
THEN ALL PEOPLE WILL KNOW ABOUT THE MIGHTY THINGS YOU HAVE DONE.
THEY WILL KNOW ABOUT THE GLORIOUS MAJESTY OF YOUR KINGDOM.
YOUR KINGDOM IS A KINGDOM THAT WILL LAST FOREVER.
YOUR RULE WILL CONTINUE FOR ALL TIME TO COME.

THE LORD WILL KEEP ALL HIS PROMISES.
HE IS FAITHFUL IN EVERYTHING HE DOES.

PSALM 145:5-13

MORE TO EXPLORE

INTRODUCING PSALMS
Psalm 40, Psalm 57:9–11, Psalm 150

INTRODUCING PROVERBS
Proverbs 1:1–7, 2 Chronicles 1:7–13, James 3:17

GOD MADE EVERYTHING
Psalm 104, Isaiah 40:25–31, Jeremiah 32:17

GOD MADE YOU
Genesis 1:26–27, Psalm 100:1–3, Psalm 119:73

GOD IS ALWAYS WITH US
Matthew 1:23, Romans 8:37–39, 1 John 4:13

WHEN LIFE IS DIFFICULT
Psalm 42, John 16:33, Romans 5:1–8, 1 Peter 5:7

GOD IS WORTHY OF PRAISE
Psalm 19:1–4, Psalm 30:11–12, Psalm 66:1–4

GOD HEARS OUR PRAYERS
Luke 5:16, Philippians 4:4–7, James 5:16

REMEMBER WHAT GOD HAS DONE
Lamentations 3:21–23, Psalm 71:15–17, Psalm 77:11–12

MORE TO EXPLORE

KEEPING GOD IN OUR THOUGHTS
Philippians 4:8, 1 Thessalonians 5:16–18, Psalm 111:2

OUR DAILY BREAD
Psalm 145:15–16, Matthew 6:25–34, Luke 11:2–4

TRUST IN GOD
Psalm 37:3–6, Romans 15:13, Isaiah 26:3–4

GOD GUIDES OUR PATH
Psalm 16:11, Psalm 23:3, Romans 12:1–2

THE LORD IS MY SHEPHERD
Psalm 95:6–7, Isaiah 40:11, John 10:14

GOD WATCHES OVER US
Psalm 16:1–2, Psalm 46:1–3, Romans 8:31

ENOUGH FOR EVERYONE
Psalm 146:5–10, Proverbs 14:21, Luke 3:11

BE GENEROUS
1 Timothy 6:17–19, 1 Peter 4:9–10, 1 John 3:16–18

LOVE YOUR ENEMIES
Matthew 5:43–44, Luke 6:27–36, Galatians 5:14

MORE TO EXPLORE

DON'T BE QUICK TO ANGER
Proverbs 14:29, Ephesians 4:31–32, 1 Thessalonians 5:15

WATCH YOUR WORDS
Proverbs 11:12–13, Proverbs 15:1–2, 4, Ephesians 4:29

BE A PEACEMAKER
James 3:17–18, Proverbs 12:20, Romans 12:18

REFLECTING GOD'S LOVE
Psalm 126:2–3, 2 Corinthians 1:3–4, 1 John 4:12

FRIENDSHIP
Proverbs 12:26, Proverbs 17:17, Ecclesiastes 4:9–12

BE HUMBLE
Matthew 5:5, Romans 12:3, Philippians 2:3–4

OTHERS HELP US GROW
Proverbs 10:17, Proverbs 18:15, Hebrews 12:11

FORGIVENESS
Luke 17:3–4, Colossians 3:12–15, 1 John 1:9

GOD SEES OUR HEARTS
Psalm 33:13–15, Proverbs 4:20–23, Luke 6:43–45

MORE TO EXPLORE

BE STILL AND KNOW
  Psalm 29:11, Psalm 62:1, Matthew 11:28–29

CARING FOR CREATION
  Genesis 2:15, Deuteronomy 10:14, Psalm 24:1

GOD LOVES WHAT IS RIGHT AND FAIR
  Proverbs 31:8–9, Isaiah 1:17, Acts 20:35

GOD IS FAITHFUL
  Deuteronomy 7:9, Psalm 145:12–13, 1 Corinthians 1:9

JOY
  Psalm 28:7, Psalm 65:8, Galatians 5:22–23

GOD IS LOVE
  Ephesians 3:18–19, 1 John 3:1, Psalm 36:5

GIVE THANKS
  2 Corinthians 9:15, Colossians 2:6–7, James 1:17